# SOUND INNOVATIONS

## ENSEMBLE DEVELOPMENT

### Chorales and Warm-up Exercises for Tone, Technique and Rhythm

## INTERMEDIATE CONCERT BAND

Peter **BOONSHAFT** | Chris **BERNOTAS**

Thank you for making *Sound Innovations: Ensemble Development* a part of your concert band curriculum. With 412 exercises, including over 70 chorales by some of today's most renowned composers for concert band, it is our hope you will find this book to be a valuable resource in helping you grow in your understanding and abilities as an ensemble musician.

An assortment of exercises are grouped by key and presented in a variety of intermediate difficulty levels. Where possible, several exercises in the same category are provided to allow for variety while accomplishing the goals of that specific type of exercise. You will notice that many exercises and chorales are clearly marked with dynamics, articulations, style, and tempo for you to practice those aspects of performance. Other exercises are intentionally left for you or your teacher to determine how best to use them in reaching your performance goals.

Whether you are progressing through exercises to better your technical facility or to challenge your musicianship with beautiful chorales, we are confident you will be excited, motivated, and inspired by using *Sound Innovations: Ensemble Development*.

**Alfred**

© 2012 Alfred Music Publishing Co., Inc.
Sound Innovations™ is a trademark of Alfred Music Publishing Co., Inc.
All Rights Reserved including Public Performance
ISBN-10: 0-7390-6774-5
ISBN-13: 978-0-7390-6774-1
Instrument photos courtesy of Yamaha Corporation of America Band & Orchestral Division

# Concert B♭ Major (Your G Major)

**1** **PASSING THE TONIC**

**2** **PASSING THE TONIC**

**3** **PASSING THE TONIC**

**4** **PASSING THE TONIC**

**5** **PASSING THE TONIC**

**6** **BREATHING AND LONG TONES**

**7** **BREATHING AND LONG TONES**

**8** **BREATHING AND LONG TONES**

**9** **BREATHING AND LONG TONES**

**CONCERT B♭ MAJOR SCALE (YOUR G MAJOR SCALE)**

**SCALE PATTERN**

**SCALE PATTERN**

**SCALE PATTERN**

**SCALE PATTERN**

**SCALE PATTERN**

**CHANGING SCALE RHYTHM**

**CONCERT B♭ CHROMATIC SCALE (YOUR G CHROMATIC SCALE)**

4

**18  FLEXIBILITY**

**19  FLEXIBILITY**

**20  ARPEGGIOS**

**21  ARPEGGIOS**

**22  INTERVALS**

**23  INTERVALS**

**24  BALANCE AND INTONATION: PERFECT INTERVALS**

**25  BALANCE AND INTONATION: DIATONIC HARMONY**

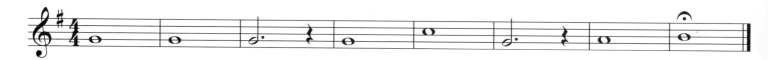

**26  BALANCE AND INTONATION: FAMILY BALANCE**

**BALANCE AND INTONATION: LAYERED TUNING**

**BALANCE AND INTONATION: MOVING CHORD TONES**

**BALANCE AND INTONATION: SHIFTING CHORD QUALITIES**

**EXPANDING INTERVALS: DOWNWARD IN PARALLEL OCTAVES**

**EXPANDING INTERVALS: DOWNWARD IN PARALLEL FIFTHS**

**EXPANDING INTERVALS: DOWNWARD IN TRIADS**

**EXPANDING INTERVALS: UPWARD IN PARALLEL OCTAVES**

**EXPANDING INTERVALS: UPWARD IN TRIADS**

**RHYTHM**

6

**36  RHYTHM**

**37  RHYTHM**

**38  RHYTHM**

**39  RHYTHM**

**40  RHYTHMIC SUBDIVISION**

**41  RHYTHMIC SUBDIVISION**

**42  RHYTHMIC SUBDIVISION**

**43  METER**

**PHRASING**

**PHRASING**

**ARTICULATION**

**DYNAMICS**

**ETUDE**

Moderately

**ETUDE**

Stately

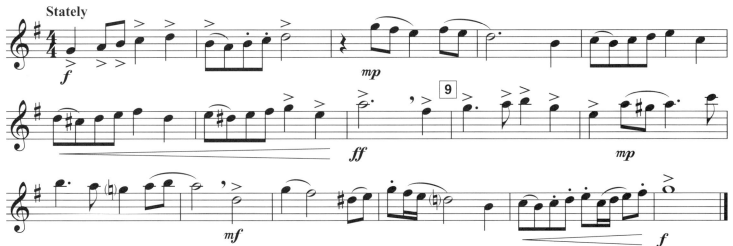

9

# Concert G Minor (Your E Minor)

**61** PASSING THE TONIC

**62** BREATHING AND LONG TONES

**63** CONCERT G NATURAL MINOR SCALE (YOUR E NATURAL MINOR SCALE)

**64** CONCERT G HARMONIC AND MELODIC MINOR SCALES

**65** SCALE PATTERN

**66** CONCERT G CHROMATIC SCALE (YOUR E CHROMATIC SCALE)

**67** FLEXIBILITY

**68** FLEXIBILITY

**69** ARPEGGIOS

**ARPEGGIOS**

**INTERVALS**

**INTERVALS**

**BALANCE AND INTONATION: DIATONIC HARMONY**

**BALANCE AND INTONATION: MOVING CHORD TONES**

**BALANCE AND INTONATION: LAYERED TUNING**

**BALANCE AND INTONATION: FAMILY BALANCE**

**EXPANDING INTERVALS: DOWNWARD IN PARALLEL FIFTHS**

**EXPANDING INTERVALS: UPWARD IN PARALLEL THIRDS**

**79 RHYTHM**

**80 RHYTHM**

**81 RHYTHM**

**82 RHYTHMIC SUBDIVISION**

**83 RHYTHMIC SUBDIVISION**

**84 ARTICULATION AND DYNAMICS**

**85 ETUDE**

13

**CHORALE**

Robert Sheldon

Larghetto

**CHORALE**

Michael Story (ASCAP)

Moderato

**CONCERT G MINOR SCALE & CHORALE**

Chris M. Bernotas (ASCAP)

**CHORALE**

Andrew Boysen, Jr.

Moderately slow, smoothly

Slower

**CHORALE**

Rossano Galante

Sad and expressive, freely

# Concert E♭ Major (Your C Major)

**91 PASSING THE TONIC**

**92 PASSING THE TONIC**

**93 PASSING THE TONIC**

**94 PASSING THE TONIC**

**95 PASSING THE TONIC**

**96 BREATHING AND LONG TONES**

**97 BREATHING AND LONG TONES**

**98 BREATHING AND LONG TONES**

**99 BREATHING AND LONG TONES**

**CONCERT E♭ MAJOR SCALE (YOUR C MAJOR SCALE)**

**SCALE PATTERN**

**SCALE PATTERN**

**SCALE PATTERN**

**SCALE PATTERN**

**SCALE PATTERN**

**CHANGING SCALE RHYTHM**

**CONCERT E♭ CHROMATIC SCALE (YOUR C CHROMATIC SCALE)**

**108** **FLEXIBILITY**

**109** **FLEXIBILITY**

**110** **ARPEGGIOS**

**111** **ARPEGGIOS**

**112** **INTERVALS**

**113** **INTERVALS**

**114** **BALANCE AND INTONATION: PERFECT INTERVALS**

**115** **BALANCE AND INTONATION: DIATONIC HARMONY**

**116** **BALANCE AND INTONATION: FAMILY BALANCE**

**BALANCE AND INTONATION: LAYERED TUNING**

**BALANCE AND INTONATION: LAYERED TUNING**

**BALANCE AND INTONATION: SHIFTING CHORD QUALITIES**

**EXPANDING INTERVALS: DOWNWARD IN PARALLEL OCTAVES**

**EXPANDING INTERVALS: DOWNWARD IN PARALLEL FIFTHS**

**EXPANDING INTERVALS: DOWNWARD IN TRIADS**

**EXPANDING INTERVALS: UPWARD IN PARALLEL OCTAVES**

**EXPANDING INTERVALS: UPWARD IN TRIADS**

**125** **RHYTHM**

**126** **RHYTHM**

**127** **RHYTHM**

**128** **RHYTHM**

**129** **RHYTHM**

**130** **RHYTHMIC SUBDIVISION**

**131** **RHYTHMIC SUBDIVISION**

**132** **RHYTHMIC SUBDIVISION**

**3 METER**

**4 PHRASING**

**5 PHRASING**

**6 ARTICULATION**

**DYNAMICS**

**ETUDE**

**ETUDE**

# Concert C Minor (Your A Minor)

**150 PASSING THE TONIC**

**151 BREATHING AND LONG TONES**

**152 CONCERT C NATURAL MINOR SCALE (YOUR A NATURAL MINOR SCALE)**

**153 CONCERT C HARMONIC AND MELODIC MINOR SCALES**

**154 SCALE PATTERN**

**155 CONCERT C CHROMATIC SCALE (YOUR A CHROMATIC SCALE)**

**156 FLEXIBILITY**

**157 FLEXIBILITY**

**ARPEGGIOS**

**ARPEGGIOS**

**INTERVALS**

**INTERVALS**

**BALANCE AND INTONATION: DIATONIC HARMONY**

**BALANCE AND INTONATION: MOVING CHORD TONES**

**BALANCE AND INTONATION: LAYERED TUNING**

**BALANCE AND INTONATION: FAMILY BALANCE**

**EXPANDING INTERVALS: DOWNWARD IN TRIADS**

**EXPANDING INTERVALS: UPWARD IN TRIADS**

24

**168** RHYTHM

**169** RHYTHM

**170** RHYTHM

**171** RHYTHMIC SUBDIVISION

**172** RHYTHMIC SUBDIVISION

**173** ARTICULATION AND DYNAMICS

**174** ETUDE

## CHORALE

Randall D. Standridge (ASCAP)

## CHORALE

Roland Barrett

## CONCERT C MINOR SCALE & CHORALE

Chris M. Bernotas (ASCAP)

## CHORALE: MEINES LEBENS LETZTE ZEIT

From the Gotha Psalter, 1726
Harmonized by J.S. Bach (1685–1750)
Arranged by Todd Stalter

Maestoso

## CHORALE

Rossano Galante

Dark and moody

26

# Concert F Major (Your D Major)

**180 PASSING THE TONIC**

**181 BREATHING AND LONG TONES**

**182 CONCERT F MAJOR SCALE (YOUR D MAJOR SCALE)**

**183 SCALE PATTERN**

**184 SCALE PATTERN**

**185 CONCERT F CHROMATIC SCALE (YOUR D CHROMATIC SCALE)**

**186 FLEXIBILITY**

**187 FLEXIBILITY**

**38  ARPEGGIOS**

**39  ARPEGGIOS**

**40  INTERVALS**

**41  BALANCE AND INTONATION: DIATONIC HARMONY**

**42  BALANCE AND INTONATION: FAMILY BALANCE**

**43  BALANCE AND INTONATION: LAYERED TUNING**

**BALANCE AND INTONATION: MOVING CHORD TONES**

**BALANCE AND INTONATION: SHIFTING CHORD QUALITIES**

**EXPANDING INTERVALS: DOWNWARD IN PARALLEL FIFTHS**

**EXPANDING INTERVALS: UPWARD IN PARALLEL FIFTHS**

**198 RHYTHM**

**199 RHYTHM**

**200 RHYTHM**

**201 RHYTHMIC SUBDIVISION**

**202 RHYTHMIC SUBDIVISION**

**203 ARTICULATION AND DYNAMICS**

**204 ETUDE**

# Concert D Minor (Your B Minor)

**210** **PASSING THE TONIC**

**211** **BREATHING AND LONG TONES**

**212** **CONCERT D NATURAL MINOR SCALE (YOUR B NATURAL MINOR SCALE)**

**213** **CONCERT D HARMONIC AND MELODIC MINOR SCALES**

**214** **SCALE PATTERN**

**215** **SCALE PATTERN**

**216** **CONCERT D CHROMATIC SCALE (YOUR B CHROMATIC SCALE)**

**217** **FLEXIBILITY**

**8** **FLEXIBILITY**

**9** **ARPEGGIOS**

**0** **ARPEGGIOS**

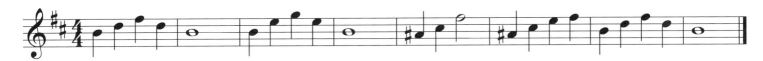

**1** **INTERVALS**

**2** **BALANCE AND INTONATION: DIATONIC HARMONY**

**3** **BALANCE AND INTONATION: FAMILY BALANCE**

**BALANCE AND INTONATION: LAYERED TUNING**

**BALANCE AND INTONATON: MOVING CHORD TONES**

**EXPANDING INTERVALS: DOWNWARD IN TRIADS**

**EXPANDING INTERVALS: UPWARD IN TRIADS**

32

**228 RHYTHM**

**229 RHYTHM**

**230 RHYTHM**

**231 RHYTHMIC SUBDIVISION**

**232 RHYTHMIC SUBDIVISION**

**233 ARTICULATION AND DYNAMICS**

**234 ETUDE**

# Concert A♭ Major (Your F Major)

**240** PASSING THE TONIC

**241** BREATHING AND LONG TONES

**242** CONCERT A♭ MAJOR SCALE (YOUR F MAJOR SCALE)

**243** SCALE PATTERN

**244** SCALE PATTERN

**245** CONCERT A♭ CHROMATIC SCALE (YOUR F CHROMATIC SCALE)

**246** FLEXIBILITY

**247** FLEXIBILITY

**ARPEGGIOS**

**ARPEGGIOS**

**INTERVALS**

**BALANCE AND INTONATION: DIATONIC HARMONY**

**BALANCE AND INTONATION: FAMILY BALANCE**

**BALANCE AND INTONATION: LAYERED TUNING**

**BALANCE AND INTONATION: MOVING CHORD TONES**

**EXPANDING INTERVALS: DOWNWARD IN PARALLEL FIFTHS**

**EXPANDING INTERVALS: UPWARD IN PARALLEL THIRDS**

**257** **RHYTHM**

**258** **RHYTHM**

**259** **RHYTHM**

**260** **RHYTHMIC SUBDIVISION**

**261** **RHYTHMIC SUBDIVISION**

**262** **DYNAMICS**

**263** **ARTICULATION AND DYNAMICS**

**264** **ETUDE**

Moderately

**CHORALE**

Randall D. Standridge (ASCAP)

38

# Concert F Minor (Your D Minor)

**270** PASSING THE TONIC

**271** BREATHING AND LONG TONES

**272** CONCERT F NATURAL MINOR SCALE (YOUR D NATURAL MINOR SCALE)

**273** CONCERT F HARMONIC AND MELODIC MINOR SCALES

**274** SCALE PATTERN

**275** CONCERT F CHROMATIC SCALE (YOUR D CHROMATIC SCALE)

**276** FLEXIBILITY

**277** FLEXIBILITY

**278** ARPEGGIOS

**ARPEGGIOS**

**INTERVALS**

**INTERVALS**

**BALANCE AND INTONATION: DIATONIC HARMONY**

**BALANCE AND INTONATION: FAMILY BALANCE**

**BALANCE AND INTONATION: LAYERED TUNING**

**BALANCE AND INTONATION: MOVING CHORD TONES**

**EXPANDING INTERVALS: DOWNWARD IN TRIADS**

**EXPANDING INTERVALS: UPWARD IN TRIADS**

**288** **RHYTHM**

**289** **RHYTHM**

**290** **RHYTHM**

**291** **RHYTHMIC SUBDIVISION**

**292** **RHYTHMIC SUBDIVISION**

**293** **ARTICULATION AND DYNAMICS**

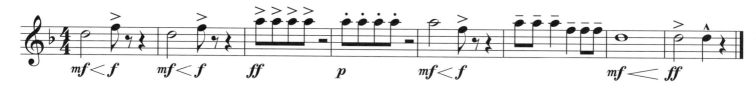

**294** **ETUDE**

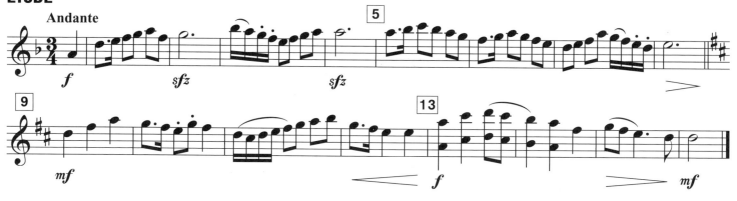

## CHORALE

Randall D. Standridge (ASCAP)

## CHORALE

Roland Barrett

## CONCERT F MINOR SCALE & CHORALE

Chris M. Bernotas (ASCAP)

## CHORALE

Robert Sheldon

**Andante**

## CHORALE

Ralph Ford (ASCAP)

**Lament**

**A tempo**

# Concert D♭ Major (Your B♭ Major)

**300**    **BREATHING AND LONG TONES**

**301**    **CONCERT D♭ MAJOR SCALE (YOUR B♭ MAJOR SCALE)**

**302**    **SCALE PATTERN**

**303**    **SCALE PATTERN**

**304**    **SCALE PATTERN**

**305**    **FLEXIBILITY**

**306**    **ARPEGGIOS**

**307**    **INTERVALS**

**BALANCE AND INTONATION: FAMILY BALANCE**

**BALANCE AND INTONATION: LAYERED TUNING**

**EXPANDING INTERVALS: DOWNWARD AND UPWARD IN PARALLEL OCTAVES**

**ARTICULATION AND DYNAMICS**

**ETUDE**

**ETUDE**

**CHORALE**

Andrew Boysen, Jr.

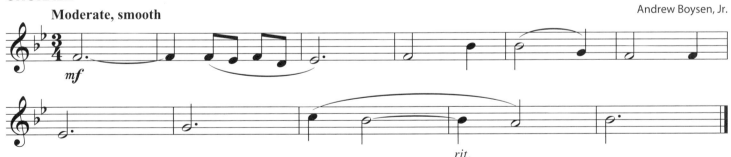

**CHORALE**

Todd Stalter

# Concert B♭ Minor (Your G Minor)

**316** **BREATHING AND LONG TONES**

**317** **CONCERT B♭ NATURAL MINOR SCALE (YOUR G NATURAL MINOR SCALE)**

**318** **CONCERT B♭ HARMONIC AND MELODIC MINOR SCALES**

**319** **SCALE PATTERN**

**320** **SCALE PATTERN**

**321** **FLEXIBILITY**

**322** **ARPEGGIOS**

**323** **INTERVALS**

**324** **BALANCE AND INTONATION: LAYERED TUNING**

## 5 BALANCE AND INTONATION: MOVING CHORD TONES

## 6 EXPANDING INTERVALS: DOWNWARD IN TRIADS

## 7 ARTICULATION AND DYNAMICS

## 8 ETUDE

Slowly

## 9 ETUDE

Dramatically

## 10 CHORALE

Michael Story (ASCAP)

Moderately slow

## 11 CHORALE

Robert Sheldon

Andante

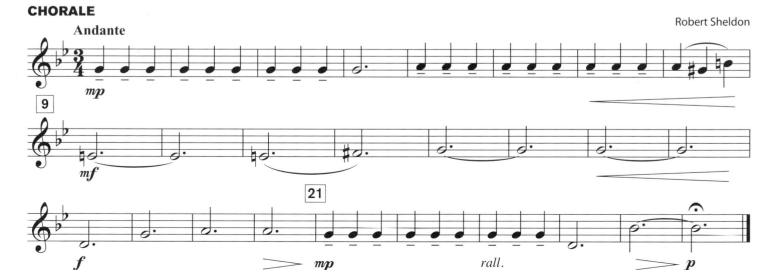

# Concert C Major (Your A Major)

**332  BREATHING AND LONG TONES**

**333  CONCERT C MAJOR SCALE (YOUR A MAJOR SCALE)**

**334  SCALE PATTERN**

**335  SCALE PATTERN**

**336  FLEXIBILITY**

**337  ARPEGGIOS**

**338  INTERVALS**

**339  INTERVALS**

**340  BALANCE AND INTONATION: FAMILY BALANCE**

47

**BALANCE AND INTONATION: LAYERED TUNING**

**EXPANDING INTERVALS: DOWNWARD IN PARALLEL FIFTHS**

**ARTICULATION AND DYNAMICS**

**ETUDE**

**ETUDE**

**CHORALE**

Ralph Ford (ASCAP)

**CHORALE: LARGO FROM THE "NEW WORLD SYMPHONY"**

Antonín Dvořák
Arranged by Michael Story (ASCAP)

# Concert A Minor (Your F# Minor)

**348** **BREATHING AND LONG TONES**

**349** **CONCERT A NATURAL MINOR SCALE (YOUR F# NATURAL MINOR SCALE)**

**350** **CONCERT A HARMONIC AND MELODIC MINOR SCALES**

**351** **SCALE PATTERN**

**352** **FLEXIBILITY**

**353** **ARPEGGIOS**

**354** **INTERVALS**

**355** **INTERVALS**

**356** **BALANCE AND INTONATION: DIATONIC HARMONY**

**BALANCE AND INTONATION: FAMILY BALANCE**

**EXPANDING INTERVALS: DOWNWARD IN TRIADS**

**ARTICULATION AND DYNAMICS**

**ETUDE**

**ETUDE**

**CHORALE**

Todd Stalter

**CHORALE**

Roland Barrett

# Concert G Major (Your E Major)

**364** **CONCERT G MAJOR SCALE (YOUR E MAJOR SCALE)**

**365** **BALANCE AND INTONATION: FAMILY BALANCE**

**366** **ETUDE**

**367** **CHORALE**

Michael Story (ASCAP)

# Concert E Minor (Your C♯ Minor)

**368** **CONCERT E NATURAL MINOR SCALE (YOUR C♯ NATURAL MINOR SCALE)**

**369** **CONCERT E HARMONIC AND MELODIC MINOR SCALES**

**370** **BALANCE AND INTONATION: LAYERED TUNING**

**371** **ETUDE**

**372** **CHORALE**

Chris M. Bernotas (ASCAP)

# Advancing Rhythm and Meter

52

**383** ⁶⁄₈ **METER**

**384** ⁶⁄₈ **METER**

**385** ⁶⁄₈ **METER**

**386** ⁶⁄₈ **METER**

**387** ⁶⁄₈ **METER**

**388** ⁶⁄₈ **METER**

**389** ⁶⁄₈ **METER**

**390** ⁶⁄₈ **METER**

**391** **CHANGING METERS:** ⁴⁄₄ **AND** ⁶⁄₈

**392** **CHANGING METERS:** ³⁄₄ **AND** ⁶⁄₈

**TRIPLETS**

**TRIPLETS**

**TRIPLETS**

**TRIPLETS**

**TRIPLETS**

**TRIPLETS**

**TRIPLETS**

**TRIPLETS**

**TRIPLETS**

**TRIPLETS**

54

# Alto Saxophone Fingering Chart

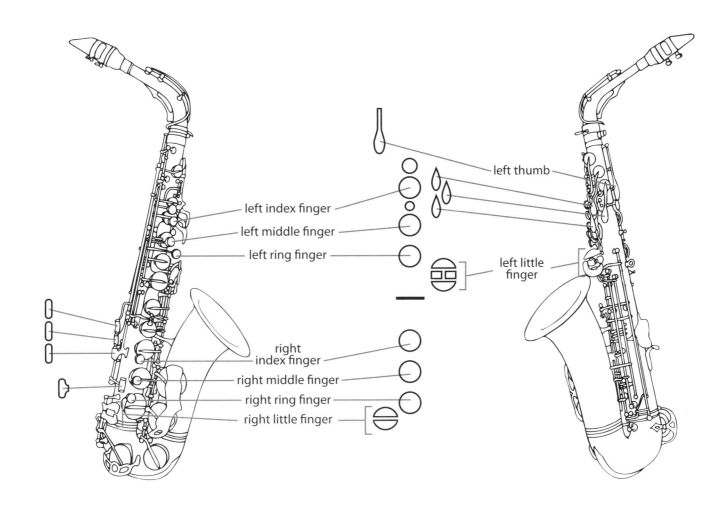

○ = open
● = pressed down

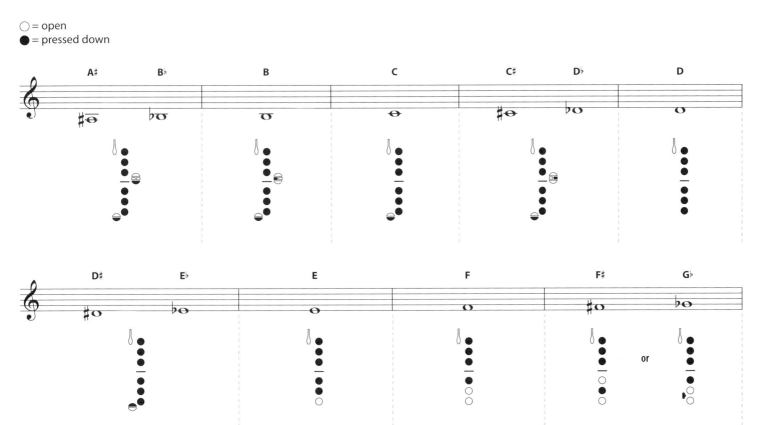

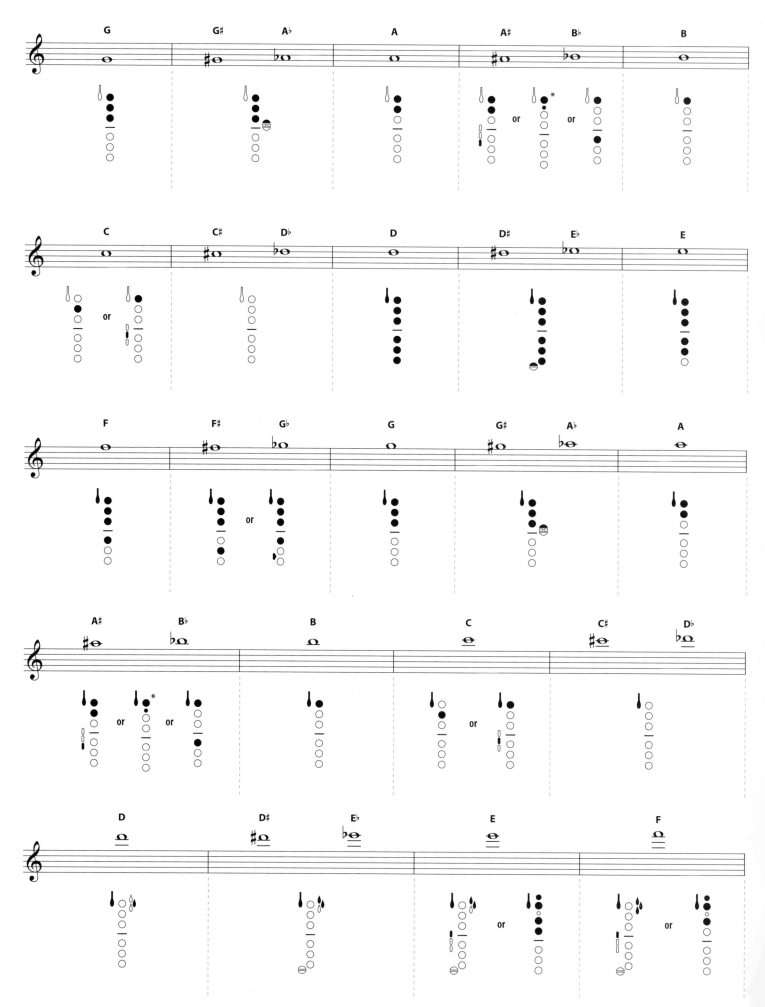

*The bis key is used for this fingering. This fingering should not be used in a chromatic scale.